Dancing with the Fairies

AMY SHINE

Dancing with the Fairies
Copyright © 2023 by Amy Shine
ISBN: 979-8-9896384-0-6 (paperback)
ISBN: 979-8-9896384-1-3 (eBook)

Published by Amy Shine
www.amyshine.net

To all the Fairies who danced with me and showed me the way from the darkness to the light.

Contents

Acknowledgements

I have so much gratitude for so many people who have influenced me and helped shape who I am today.

To my mother, Kathryn Shine: thank you for believing in magic and never giving up on us. To my Dad: Pat Shine, thank you for showing me what it is to be a wild Irish rover and never shutting that down. Thank you both for letting me spread my wings and never stopping me.

Shannon O'Hara, thank you for bringing Talk to the Entities to the world and educating me and others with such pragmatic information about the Spirit World.

Thank you Earth for being my greatest teacher.

And thank you to all my fairy sisters and fairy friends, you know who you are.

CHAPTER 1:

Growing Up in a World of Fairies

I reland is a land of green. In fact, there are more trees in Ireland than people. It may still be one of the few places on this Earth that acknowledges the Fairies that are actively part of the Earth's energy.

I grew up in Ireland, a land where we honor the Fairies by never building on fairy forts. A fairy fort is an earthen mound often marked by stones in the shape of a circle showing the remains of where druids once lived. The belief is that if you build on them, you will disturb the magic there and be cursed.

Even though this is all part of the Irish way of living, no one really talks much about the Fairies anymore. My mother would talk to me about them when I was little as she read books to me, but as I grew up and became a serious adult, I would never hear anyone really talk about the Fairies. Yet, everyone would tell you to protect the fairy forts and don't you dare try to build on them.

If the people in Ireland did not believe in Fairies, why then would they protect the fairy forts? No... yet they do.

What I know now after studying the world of consciousness, magic, and the spirit world for the last 10 years, is that there are many Fairies and Nature spirits of different kinds in Ireland. The people there may not talk about it but you can definitely perceive them if you are willing to expand your senses beyond the physical!

As I've travelled through the world to different parts of Nature, forests and mountains, I've found that the Fairies are still present in many parts although the people may have forgotten.

I spent many years dancing with the Fairies on the land in Ireland, in the forests, and on the cliffs. I just didn't acknowledge their presence at that time.

When I started really going on the journey of consciousness through Access Consciousness® and Talk to the Entities® classes, it really put words to things I had always been aware of, but never had been able to acknowledge.

The conversations in Talk to the Entities classes about Spirits of the Earth really gave me a language and awareness of the Nature spirits and Fairies that if I had not found it, would never have allowed me to acknowledge the magic I accessed when I danced with the Earth.

I also started to read other books out in the world like myths and mythology of Fairies. With the tools of Talk to the Entities, I was really able to identify what was true for me and what was a lie.

The more I questioned and the more I danced with the Earth, the more I strengthened the communion I had with the Fairies. (As crazy as this may sound, the Fairies asked me to write this book.)

Since you picked this book up and you might be looking for a different possibility and communion with the Nature spirits and Fairies, it is my hope you may be inspired by the tools in this book and go on your own journey of discovery to include all the Nature spirits and Fairies in your life.

The land in Ireland is alive and luscious and so are the Fairies if you are willing to throw your logical, thinking mind away and go deep into the forest and mountains there.

Are you willing to ask to perceive them?

CHAPTER 2:

Education of the Spirit World

You can't communicate with the Fairies through your mind. You have to throw your logical mind away.

You also don't want to focus on trying to "see" the Fairies. Your sight is limited.

Instead of thinking, ask: "What do I know?"

Instead of trying to feel, ask: "What am I perceiving?"

Instead of trying to see, ask: "What am I sensing?"

Try this:

Go out in Nature and ask to perceive the Fairies.

Ask the Fairies to make their presence known to you. Ask them to come back from where they have retreated and touch you, tickle you.

What do you perceive?

How many times have you been in Nature, where the Fairies have whispered at you, brushed lightly on your face, flickered at you, and you have ignored it?

What if you stopped ignoring those subtle perceptions of awareness you perceive? Will you allow yourself to perceive that again? Will you acknowledge what you do perceive and ask for more to show up?

Are the Fairies solid and physical with bodies or are they energetic and subtle?

What do you know?

So once again, throw your mind away.

Let go of the need to see the Fairies through the lens of this calculating, physical reality.

Let the Fairies tickle you, flicker at you, dance with you.

Ask them to show you their presence and all the ways you perceive them that you've never acknowledged before.

Perceiving the Fairies Exercise:

Ask all the Fairies that you have dismissed and not acknowledged to come back to you.

Ask them to show you when they are present with you.

Take a breath.

Soften.

Relax.

What do you perceive?

What are you aware of?

Are the Fairies with you right now?

What are the very subtle ways they show you they are?

Dancing with the Fairies Meditation 1:

Inhale into your body, feel your belly rise up into your heart.

Exhale, drop out of your mind and into your body.

All the wisdom of the Earth and the Nature spirits lies in your body.

Get really present with your body.

How does your body feel today?

Do you have any nervousness? Anxiety? Mind racing?

Feel your body and allow yourself to be in your body.

Your body comes from the Earth.

When you disconnect from your body, you disconnect from the Earth and all the Nature spirits.

Use your breath to bring you back to your body. Feel your feet touching into the Earth and push your mind out of the way as you expand into the Earth with your body.

Can you come back to the root system with the Earth?

Let the roots of your feet expand down into the root system of the Earth.

Can you go deep down in the Earth and start to perceive the Fairies of the Earth?

Everything has a spirit: the trees, the soil beneath you, the mountains.

Is there a particular fairy that would like to work with you today?

Notice if an energy pops, something drops into your head or pings in your world.

Invite that energy/fairy spirit to be with you today.

Relax.

What do you perceive about this fairy?

What kind of fairy energy is this?

Would you be willing to receive any wisdom this fairy has to share with you today, that can facilitate you?

Perceive this fairy's energy, acknowledge them, do they have a name?

What is their energy like?

Invite/allow them to sit with you as you lay on/with the Earth, ask them to facilitate you today.

You can ask the Fairies to have more clarity on anything you are unclear with.

What is asking to be changed in your world? Personal life?

What is asking to be changed in the world that this fairy spirit is here to show you?

What are they asking for you to sit in stillness with?

How could you honor your earth body today?

Reaching into this fairy spirit's world, asking them to show you.

How can we honor the Earth?

How can we honor the Nature spirits and Fairies?

Relax and ask them to show you.

What ways of Mother Earth have been lost?

What has been lost with the Earth and also with you?

Go deep down into Earth and into the earth body.

What is asking to be planted in your world and in the world right now?

Thank the fairy spirit for being and showing up for this meditation today. Thank the Earth, yourself and your body.

You can also journal any messages or energies that came through in this meditation.

CHAPTER 3:

When Did You Stop Believing in Fairies and Magic?

I was born in a small town called Mallow in County Cork. The house I spent my first few years in was at the top of a mountain road that was surrounded by forest and trees. I had two older brothers who I adored and spent as much time as I could following them around.

I also loved to just play by myself. I would make up my own games, set up shop in the garden, make tree houses, and spend every hour of light outside in nature. It looked like I was playing by myself yet, in my world, I was never alone. I had, what I know now, so many energies around me that skipped, played, hopped, jumped, and danced with me. I didn't have to define them as "Fairies," because until the age of three, I didn't have any need to define anything.

How old were you when you first started to shut down your awareness of the Fairies?

I started to cut off my awareness of the Fairies at about three years old, when I tried to understand the world around me. If you look at the word itself, when you try to understand you must "stand under" what another person believes and you lose sight of what may be true for you. You think if you could just understand them, then you would see why they choose what they choose. This need to understand the world around us then takes us out of our magical world and keeps us stuck in the insane beliefs of others'.

Did you try to understand the world or people around you which then has kept you locked out of your magical world?

If you have done that, first acknowledge you chose that. Now would you be willing to let that go?

Make the demand of yourself and then request of the Earth and the Fairies that you have the communion that you once had before you chose to give it up.

What did you know even as a child?

Do you ever see how babies look all around you? They can see all the colors around you; they see you. They also perceive all the energies, both embodied and dis-embodied, and that includes the spirit world, angels, Fairies and anything else that is either physical or non-physical.

They just don't define it!

I had so much fun playing as a child because I played with all the energies around me.

How many of you played with all different energies as a child and had no judgment or definition of what they were?

How old were you when you gave up what you knew and your ability to sense and see all energies around you for feeling, thinking and understanding?

I gave it all up completely when I turned nine years old. Which is interesting, since that is usually the age when you start to make judgment real.

At nine years old, I stopped playing. I put my toys away and decided I needed to be a grown up.

I gave up on the world of Fairies, play, fun, curiosity, joy and wonder at nine years old to make being an adult and fitting in more important.

How old were you when you gave up completely on the Fairies to make fitting into this world more real?

Get present with that question and see what age comes up.

Whose reality were you validating by giving up on the world of the Fairies and magic?

When you ask this question, you are not looking for an answer…just an awareness. It may be an energetic awareness.

It may also be a more cognitive awareness.

We tend to give up our magic, to make our family's reality or the world around us real.

You might not have a memory of that moment in your past when you gave up on your world of magic and Fairies yet you will have a knowing that is energetic.

It may even have been another lifetime.

Maybe you were persecuted in another lifetime for being in communion with the Fairies.

Go with the energy and acknowledge what is true for you.

I know I gave up on my world of magic, play and wonder with the Fairies when I was nine years old, because I had decided that I had to grow up and be an adult. I could no longer be a child. I remember putting my dolls away and deciding that I could no longer play.

What if you never had to give up being the child you are? What if play, wonder, curiosity, joy and adventure were the elements that invited the Fairies to be with you?

Which world would you like to live in? The serious one, where you can only be an adult and be in your head, thinking and trying to understand and control everything? Or the one of play and wonder where everyday is an adventure and you get to live in a world of oneness, communion with the Earth, and all the elementals that include all the Spirits of the Earth and the Fairies?

Did you make a decision in this lifetime or any other lifetime that separated you from your world of communion with the Fairies?

Did you make someone else's reality more important than yours and dismiss your awareness and knowing of the Fairies?

If you did that, please first acknowledge that, get present with the energy you may be stuck with and allow it to release now. Let it move from your body and being.

CHAPTER 4:

Dancing with the Fairies

How did dance bring me back to the Fairies? I was 21 years old when I was given a mental diagnosis and put on anti-psychotic medication. It was a very dark few years and the medication made me numb and dead inside.

It was my third year on medication and I had managed, through my persistence, to get weaned down on the dosage I was prescribed.

I was starting to get my energy back again, starting to have a sense of hope and wonder again.

I had always loved going clubbing and dancing and now that I wasn't drinking anymore, I started to dance at home by myself.

It started in my room. I'd find music that moved my emotions, put my headphones on and just move. Then I started to move to the deck outside and that slowly progressed to the golf course that was next to my parents' house.

I'd wait until the golfers were gone in the evenings and go out onto the green. The green would go on for miles, surrounded by trees, no traffic, no people and no noise.

Just me, barefoot on the hilly green that opened up into more green and more green and more green.

I would start off in my head, playing music and just stiffly moving my body. After a few songs, I'd find myself really letting go and moving more freely, without any thought of anything else.

At this time in my life, my mind tormented me.

This movement started to change me.

I would pick music that allowed me to move the pent up emotion in me: the sadness, the anger, the frustration… I'd find all different types of songs that moved all different types of emotions.

Once I danced it out, got the anger and frustrations out, I'd start to move with this flow. It was like I was a ballerina.

It was in the lyrical part that I started to have all sorts of fairy-like movement show up from within me.

I would swirl, twirl and just move with this grace and lightness.

Everything in my world would get lighter and brighter.

I had this sense that anything was possible.

I could create anything.

It wasn't like I was dancing by myself now… like when I first came out there.

I wasn't alone in my head now.

I was fully embodied with the Earth.

It was like a universe was dancing with me.

I started to see the world as dancing in oneness.

There was no separation, no judgment, no exclusion. All beings were included.

The Fairies were there.

I didn't see them with my eyes.

They were dancing with me energetically.

They were whispering possibilities in my ear.

They were downloading everything that I could be and choose.

They were showing me the way.

At that time, I didn't know that this was the Fairies. Now I know. From asking questions, I have come to know their energies, and now I can acknowledge what that was for me all those years ago.

It took me many years to acknowledge my knowing. I kept thinking other people saw more than me, knew more than me, were greater than me.

Do you do this? Do you make other people's experiences or awareness greater than your own? Do you dismiss what you know because you've decided someone else knows more than you?

What if you had your own awareness and connection with the Fairies that is not like anyone else's?

What if you never had to explain or justify that knowing to anyone else, only acknowledge it for you?

What is required to dance with Fairies?

The more you engage with the energy of the Fairies, the more your body becomes vital, verdant and alive just like the Earth.

Dancing with the Fairies is moving beyond control, beyond definition, dancing beyond your form and structure, your right and wrong and that is where the true magic lies.

When you can let go of right and wrong, of judgment, of structure and really surrender and allow your body to really let go of control, that is when the chaos of the Universe moves within you. Everything has rhythm, nothing is ordered and controlled, and you begin to access a whole world of magic beyond your mind.

That is where all the magic happens. That is where we get to access these subtle energies of the Earth, of the Fairies, of the spirit world, of what is actually true for you.

What is light is actually what is true for you, what is space is what is true for you. Form, structure, significance, control: that is all a human construct, a human reality.

The Earth doesn't function from form, structure and control. The Earth is out of control and the

Fairies are part of the Earth's energy and they are out of control also.

Dance with the Fairies Movement Meditation

When you are ready, connect your feet down into the Earth.

Take an inhale into your body. Maybe touch your body.

Soften.

Relax your mind.

Now invite back all the Fairies you have ever known in any lifetime.

Invite back any Fairies you have known on any earth or from any embodiment.

Don't try to see them.

Perceive them.

Lower your walls. Lower your barriers.

Push down all the filters you have been using to separate you from the subtle energetics of the Fairies.

Now invite the Fairies to move through you.

Start to circle into your body.

Move your head in a circular motion. Then move your shoulders in circles.

Move the circles into the front of your heart and back of your heart.

Move the circles down into your hips, legs and feet.

What if you didn't have to move your body from your mind?

What if you could allow the fairy energy to move through you? Allow your fingers and your arms to open up.

Close your eyes.

Inhaling down into the Earth, scooping energy from the Earth, pulling up through your feet, your legs, up through your body, up and out through the crown of your head.

Circling your movement down into the Earth, activating the element of earth and then circling up into your sacrum. Circling through the spine.

If you start yawning, belching, coughing, just know that your body starts to detox when you begin conscious movement. When you drop into your body and get present, your body starts letting go of stuck energy.

Pull energy from the core of the Earth up through the back of your legs, the back of your sacrum, holding it here in your sacrum, activating the power in your sacrum, pulling that energy through the back of your spine, flow it out through the crown of your head, opening up your crown and flow out into the Universe.

Keep it moving, keep it flowing, circling through your whole body.

Take a moment and ask to receive the Fairies' energies again.

What can the Fairies' energies facilitate for you today?

Let the Fairies move through you.

Bring in the element of water, like your moving water through the air.

Allow the water energy to move through your fingers.

You are spiraling your fingers in the air and let the spirits of the water facilitate you here and move through you.

Bring in that fluidity of movement.

What have you been trying to get right, correct and perfect that is creating stagnation and control in your body and in your life?

The Fairies don't live in a world of order and control.

Start to bring that spiral motion, through your hands and into your shoulders, into the back of your shoulder blades.

Slow, sensual movement.

Spiraling and undulating with the water spirits, from the oceans and the rivers, through every single cell in your body.

What can the Fairies facilitate through you if you would allow yourself to surrender your control?

Letting that spiral movement flow through you with no control.

No thinking. Just moving.

Body show me.

Fairies show me.

Give them permission to override your mind.

Let your hips go, let your spine go, let your sacrum go.

Expanding out even more now.

Taking up more space.

Stretching yourself even further out into the Universe, across all the earths you've ever known.

How many Fairies are you connected to from all lifetimes that you can invite back to create with you, engage with you and work with you in this lifetime?

Ask them to show you that they are here with you.

Begin to recognize and acknowledge the subtle ways they are showing you and your body that they are here.

Be with them.

Push your thinking mind out of the way.

Ask the Fairies to show you what is required of you to live in communion with them and the Earth?

What are you currently choosing that separates you from living in a world with the Fairies?

Ask the Fairies to show you how you have been blocking them in your life and give them permission to intervene when you separate from them.

What can the Fairies facilitate for you and through you?

What can you facilitate for the Fairies?

What do you and your body require to cleanse that would allow you to live in a world with the Fairies?

What small changes are the Fairies asking you to make in your day to start including their energies throughout everyday?

Sit out in Nature and ask the Fairies to show you.

Journal, write and see what comes up!

Living in a world with the Fairies is going to require us to push ourselves beyond the distractions of this reality, beyond the thinking, the doing and the busyness.

We are rewiring our being, our bodies and our way of being in the world.

If we want to live in a world with Fairies, we have to rewire not only our bodies and our being, but our way of being in the world.

CHAPTER 5:

The Power of Dancing with the Earth and Embodiment

I f you'd like to have a deeper connection to the Fairies and Nature spirits, you first have to embody.

You cannot have a communion with the Fairies from your mind.

That's why movement was so powerful in facilitating me to access so much of their magic.

Movement facilitated me out of my crazy thinking head and into my body... and that got me moving with the Earth's energy.

What can facilitate you out of your mind, beyond your control systems and into your body and the Earth?

When you are willing to let go of your mind, drop into your body, let go of control and move with the Earth, that is where the magic and mysteries will be.

How much do you avoid choosing anything that would facilitate this for you?

Here are some suggestions for getting out of your head and into your body:

- Walking barefoot on the Earth
- Dancing barefoot on grass or outside near trees or on the beach
- Finding any Ecstatic Dance, Chakra Dance or conscious dance movement class that moves you out of your head
- Playing music and moving your body freely without judgment
- Receiving an energy work session that gets you out of your head.
- Receiving any bodywork, massage or energy work where your body is being touched like Access Bars®, InnerDance or Reiki.

So much of accessing this world of Fairies is based on your willingness to receive.

In order to receive, you first have to let go of your control.

What can you choose everyday that would invite you to let go of more and more control?

Remember control is anywhere you are trying to be right or wrong.

When I danced with the Earth, there was no right or wrong in the movement. That was the first place where I began to let go of control.

This is your invitation to explore what that is for you.

Letting Go of Control Exercise:

Ask the Earth and the Fairies to show you all the places you are trying to be right or wrong and choosing to control. (Watch out for what might show up!!)

Ask the Earth and the Fairies to show you the way to embody and let go of control.

Ask the Earth and the Fairies to show you what you can choose that would facilitate that for you.

For me, it was movement; for you it may be something else. It could be singing, painting, writing, gardening, cooking or something else.

Ask for it and it will show up.

CHAPTER 6:

What Are the Lies We Have Bought and Sold About Fairies?

Lie: Fairies will get mad at you and seek revenge if you do something to upset them.

Truth: Fairies don't live in a world of right and wrong.

In other words, they don't judge you.

In my research and reading about Fairies from different books in the world, I found some of what was written about the Fairies made me feel heavy and wasn't true for me.

Questions I asked to get more awareness:

- "What is the lie here about Fairies?"
- "Fairies, what is true here?"
- "Is what is written about you actually true?"

The information the Fairies gave me is that they don't live in a world of judgment.

There is no right or wrong in a fairy's world.

Fairies are part of the Earth's energy. They are part of the Earth's biology and make up.

In her specialty class Spirits of the Earth, Shannon O' Hara ,creator and founder of Talk to the Entities, talks about how human reality likes to make everything that is different or that doesn't fit into human constructs appear as human to understand it, control it and limit it.

Her question is: "Are Fairies really little invisible ladies running around in Nature with wings or are they the humanization of the consciousness of Nature?"

So when you talk to the Fairies, what if you could let go of any definition or idea you have in your mind of how they should appear or look?

In fact, your sight is limited. What if your willingness to perceive the Fairies and their subtle energies was far superior to trying to see with your eyes?

The Fairies may appear to some of you as little women with wings as a way for you to receive them.

Would it also be easier if you didn't have to see the Fairies and allowed yourself to instead perceive/ sense them?

Communing with the Fairies Exercise :

(If you can do this exercise while out in Nature or sitting next to a tree, please do. If not, just ask to be with the Earth energetically.)

Take a deep breath into your body.

On the inhale, let your chest rise.

On the exhale, let your chest fall and your whole nervous system relax.

Take another breath and relax your mind.

Let every muscle in your body soften.

Relax some more.

Go deep down into the Earth, deep into the soil.

Go deep into the forests.

Go deep into the mountains.

Ask the Fairies to be here with you.

Lower any walls or barriers you have up that you don't even know you have up.

Ask the Fairies that occupy the trees and forests if they would be willing to make their presence known to you.

Perceive/Sense them.

Ask them to touch you, tickle you; let you know they are here.

Relax some more; lighten up.

Let go of anywhere you are making this serious or significant. Fairies do not live in a world of significance or seriousness.

What do you perceive/sense?

What gentle awareness are they being here with you?

Acknowledge what you perceive.

Get to know the energies of the Fairies.

The more you acknowledge the Fairies' presence, the more you can receive from them.

Ask them questions.

What do they know about you?

What do you know about them?

What gift can you now be for them?

What gift can they be for you?

Ask them to show you the way for creating a brighter, lighter world where the Earth and all the Spirits of the Earth are included?

Thank them for being here.

(Come back to this exercise whenever you desire and each time you will have a different awareness and experience.)

Lie: If you ask the Fairies for something, you then owe them.

Truth: Fairies don't live in a world of give and take.

Fairies live in a world of gifting and receiving.

Does the Earth judge?

Does the ocean judge that if you swim in the water, you then owe something to the oceans?

Then, would the Fairies really have the point of view that if you ask something from them, you must then give something back in return?

That concept is the give and take from our human world.

The Fairies don't live in a human world.

They don't function from the give/take system that humans do.

The Fairies live in a world of gifting and receiving just like the Earth.

As you receive the Fairies beyond the constructs of your mind you also simultaneously gift to the Fairies.

The more you can practice receiving the Fairies beyond a world of judgment, the greater gift you can be to the Fairies.

Chapter 7

What Are Ways You Can Engage the Fairies?

Plant Gardens

Fairies like when you take care of the Earth. If you'd like to have more communion with the Fairies, add more plants to your home. Create a little garden or plant trees and/or flowers.

You could also create a Fairy garden and invite them to come visit.

You will find more connection to the Fairies the more nature you are surrounded by.

Where I grew up in Ireland, there is a mountain walk that I used to run on when I lived there. It has many deep burrows that are all woodland and trees where you can sense the Fairies and Nature spirits if you allow yourself to wonder!

The Fairies are there; you just have to start talking to them, asking them questions, engaging them and acknowledging them.

They may not talk to you in a linear human way, they may respond to you energetically and so pay attention to that and acknowledge it when it happens.

Keep the Earth Clean and be a Contribution to the Earth

Pick up rubbish. The Fairies' job is to ensure the Earth continues to thrive and often when I would see rubbish on the ground, I would hear a little voice to pick it up.

What contribution can we all be to the Earth and the Fairies in creating a clean Earth that creates a sustainable future?

You don't have to judge the people who may have littered. You don't have to fight to save the Earth. The Earth doesn't need to be saved. You also don't have to ignore what is in front of you. You can be a contribution in the smallest ways.

Play, Dance, Get Curious

Like mentioned earlier in this book, the Fairies live in a world of play, wonder, curiosity and joy.

If you'd like to connect more with the Fairies, lighten up!

Stop taking everything so seriously!

Ask to be the energy you were when you were a young child before you decided you needed to be a grown up!

Ask to have that childlike wonder again.

Get curious.

Ask questions.

The Fairies live from question, not conclusion.

When I talk to the Fairies, they often communicate that we are much too serious and don't play and have true fun and joy enough. We make things so serious and the Fairies don't understand this world of seriousness!

Dance

Dancing from a space of no judgment is a great way to connect with not only the Fairies, but also all light beings of consciousness.

When you let go of your mind, drop from your head into your body, and start to move your body with curiosity and playfulness, you can begin to access all the light energies that exist beyond your mind.

The Nature spirits and the Fairies are part of the Earth's energy.

Your body comes from the Earth.

What movement can facilitate you out of your mind and into your body that allows you to embody all of the Earth's energies including the Fairies'?

Find some music that is joyful and light.

Go out in your garden, to the beach, or anywhere in nature, and move your body with the Earth.

Use music and the movement to awaken your true joy again.

(If you find this difficult to do by yourself, please go to https://www.amyshine.net/movement and download our free 30-minute "Dance with the Earth Elements" introduction class.)

Spend time with the Trees

Some of the trees on this Earth have been around longer than us and have so much wisdom and healing energy to share. Pay attention when you see trees.

What kind of shapes do you see in the trees?

Fairies can sometimes show themselves through the trees. The Fairies in the trees may appear through different shapes.

Acknowledge what you see and the presence of the Fairies in the trees will grow stronger.

Would you be willing to sit with your back against the tree trunk for at least 20-minutes?

Give your body time to relax and allow your nervous system to be reset with the energy from the tree.

Ask the tree questions. Ask to receive wisdom from the tree and the Fairies of the tree.

What do the trees have to gift you?

What can you receive from the trees?

What knowledge and wisdom do the tree and the Fairies of the tree have for you?

What can you be for the trees and the Fairies of the trees?

The awareness may come as words, images or just subtle energies. The more you are willing to open up and allow whatever is there to come through without having to make sense or understand it from your mind, the more you will be able to receive.

CHAPTER 8:

What Are the Nature Sprits and Spirits of the Earth

I have used different terms in this book. Spirits of the Earth, also known as Nature spirits, are what we refer to as Fairies, elves, trolls, devas, spirits, mermaids and others mentioned in the fairy tales we grew up reading.

Different cultures have different Nature spirits that they are more familiar with.

Spirits of the Earth and the Fairies are part of the Earth's energy.

They are here to ensure the Earth thrives.

You will feel more connection to the Nature spirits in Nature.

After much exploration I have found that the Spirits of the Earth are more energetic than the physical image I was taught through stories and books.

My hope for you is that this book contributes to you going on your own discovery of what the Spirits of the Earth and the Fairies are for you.

What do you know?

What is true for you?

What can you uncover about you and the Fairies when you question from wonder and curiosity?

The minute you come to a conclusion about the Fairies, you cut off your communion with the Fairies. They can not be defined.

They are undefinable.

CHAPTER 9:

How Do You Know When You're Dancing/ Communing With the Fairies?

Here are some indicators you are communing with the Fairies:

- Your world gets lighter and brighter
- You have a sense of play and wonder
- You have a sense of possibilities
- You have a lightness in your body and in your movement
- Sparkles flow through your world, movement or space
- You're aware of flickers, wisps or subtle touches on your body or in your space

Please ask questions. This list is just a few indicators but definitely not an answer. You have to ask questions to get your own awareness.

What am I aware of right now?

Nothing is solid in the world of the Fairies, so stay in question.

What is this?

Who is communicating with me?

Is this the Fairies?

What are the Fairies asking of me?

What contribution can I be to the Fairies?

What can I receive here?

Keep asking questions, stay curious, stay light and have fun.

What is possible now in creating a world that includes the Fairies, the Earth and all the spirits of the Earth, seen or unseen?

Movement Meditation with the Fairies

(If you'd like the video and audio of this movement meditation, please go to www.amyshine. net/dancingwiththefairies.)

Inhale. Touch down into the Earth and get really present with it.

Pull the Earth's energy into the left side of your body. Waking up the left side of your body, up into your heart and then stretching it out into the Universe.

Now do the same for the right side of your body.

Inhale. Reach down and pull from the center of the Earth. It is like we are pulling from the core of Mother Earth. Pulling up through your body and opening up into the sky.

Reach up into the sky, pulling the golden light of the sun down through your crown, down your body and flowing it out through your feet.

Spiraling energy through your feet, through your knees, into your sacrum, letting your sacrum flow, then moving it up your spine.

As you flow energy in, you flow energy out. There is no lack in the Universe.

Start to tap into the sense of abundance in the Universe, and in the Fairies' world. Do they have any lack in their world?

As you flow energy in, energy comes from everywhere. As you flow energy out there is no lack of energy.

Start to flow that energy from everywhere and allow the Fairies to show you the energy of living in a world with no lack.

The energy is coming from everywhere, pulling it back to you with energy coming from behind you as you receive from your past. Get the energy of all the Fairies you've known in any lifetime, on any planet, in any embodiment, in any spirit world. Invite them back to be with you now.

Calling them back, pinging into their worlds, invite them to engage with you again. Ask them to show you all the ways they can communicate with you. Don't try to see them, perceive them.

How many different fairy energies from your past would like to create and work with you again?

Perceive their energies and energetic downloads from them.

Perceive all the energies they have available to facilitate you and the Earth.

What questions can you ask them? What different ways can you engage them?

Flowing this energy through your spine, through the back of you.

As you flow that energy through, pull at all the Fairies you will create with in the future. Ping into their worlds. Ping them energetically and ask to receive from all the future Fairies you will create with. All the Fairies that you will learn from and all the Fairies you will also assist.

What can they show you? What are their sounds? What are their movements? Can you allow them to move through you?

Can you lose this reality? Can you let this reality slip away and flip into the world with the Fairies?

Swirling energy from everywhere. From behind you, from the right side of you, left side of you, from the front of you, up the front side of you and from above you.

Pulling from the sky, from the heavens, from the Universe and through the Universe.

Allowing the Universe in. Allowing your body to move like a light fairy body.

Ask the Fairies to show you what it is to move as a light body, as a light energy. What is it like to move like you're flying?

Moving through the air, flowing with an ease and gracefulness and no effort?

Ask the Fairies of the air to show that.

Where have you been trying to make life hard and difficult?

Ask the Fairies to show you your light body, your fairy body and your wings.

All of you who had your wings cut off, and who had your magic in your wings and have forgotten your magic, can you release that pain and trauma now and ask for your wings and magic energetically to come back to you now?

How light is your body?

How light could your body be?

Come back to stillness. Melting down into the Earth. Let the Earth hold you like a blanket.

Sense the Fairies and the subtle ways they're showing you there here. The flickers on your face. The wind. The sounds. The birds. The sounds in the air. Acknowledge the Fairies. And the soft, subtle ways they are communing with you.

What are the ways that you can work together with the Fairies to create a lighter, brighter, luscious

Earth and world? Will you allow the Fairies to work through you?

Let these energies integrate into your body and system.

Become familiar with the energies of the Fairies, and acknowledge their presence and their presence here on this Earth.

Keep engaging with them throughout your day.

Stay connected to them and to the Earth.

Pushing yourself beyond the distractions of your mind and this world.

Turn to the silence.

Turn to the lightness.

And to the play.

Fairies live in a world with play.

What play can you add to your life, to your day, to your body that would allow you to have more fairy-play and magic?

If you have forgotten how to play, ask the Fairies to show you what play could be for you.

Conclusion

What have you always known about the Fairies?

What have the Fairies always known about you?

Have the Fairies always been with you?

Is it time to acknowledge that?

How can you incorporate fairy magic in your everyday life?

The more I acknowledge the Fairies in my world, the more magical my life becomes.

I wonder what acknowledging the Fairies would contribute to you?

Are you willing to be so different and go on the journey of discovering what it would be like to live in a world with the Fairies?

Would you like to discover a whole new world of play, magic, wonder and possibilities? What if all you have to do is ask and let go of control?

Fairies in Taiwan

(Channeled from the Fairies deep in the mountains of Taiwan to Amy, August 2023)

Go deep into the Earth,
We are here,
Deep within the mountains,
And in the trees,
You will not see us through your physical eyes,
You will feel us through your senses,
Call on us and we will come,
We used to live amongst you many moons ago,
Now many of us are sleeping.
Just like so many of you are asleep.
We are waiting for you to wake.
The more you build on the Earth, your concrete buildings,
The more our energy weakens.
The more you exclude us,
The sicker we become.
You can include us,
Call on us,
Ask us, consult us,
And we will come.
We can work together to create a lighter world.
The Earth can provide for all your needs.
We are not a myth,
We are not some childhood fairytale,

We are an organism,
Living, part of the whole.
Your mind will never understand this,
Yet your body knows,
Your body holds wisdom.
Go within,
Come back to your true nature,
To the Earth,
Return to the Soil,
The trees, the mountains, the waters,
You will find us there,
Waiting for you,
For your call,
For your questions.
Remember who you are,
Before the world told you who you are,
Come back to the childlike wonder,
Come back to your curiosity,
Come back to your true joy,
You will find us living there,

The Fairies.

About the Author

Amy Shine grew up in Ireland and moved to Florida, USA in her late twenties to live in the sunshine and create a life beyond her wildest dreams.

Amy is a mindset, energy & movement coach who loves to inspire others to awaken the joy and sensualness of their bodies.

Amy helps people change limited beliefs that are keeping them in survival in their minds, release trauma and pain and come back to pleasure with their bodies.

When you can embody pleasure: you can receive from the Earth and all the spirits of the Earth as well as access all the magic and divine wisdom within you. Your relationships become greater, you become more creative and your body becomes healthy, orgasmic and alive. Pleasure is your birthright.

Amy is an Embodied Movement & Trauma Informed Body & Spirit World Facilitator using Somatic Movement practices, sound & breathwork, chakra healing, bodywork, EMDR, Access Consciousness and advanced energetics in her classes and practices.

Amy's vision is to live in a world of Oneness where body, mind, soul and earth are all in harmony and life is a dance. She invites you to a world of magic embodied.

Free Resources

Find free resources from Amy Shine here:

YouTube Channel: www.youtube.com/amyshine1

Free Content in Private Facebook Group: https://www.facebook.com/groups/dancetooneness/

Find Amy's Podcast "The Dance to Oneness Podcast" here:
https://podcasts.apple.com/us/podcast/the-dance-to-oneness/id1526899041

Follow Amy on Instagram: www.instagram.com/amyshine.energy

Receive the free gift "Daily Energy Clearings, Activations & Manifestations" from Amy's website when you subscribe to our mailing list: www.amyshine.net

Receive a free taster "Dancing with the Earth Elements" with Amy here: https://www.amyshine.net/movement

Things Mentioned in the Book

Access Consciousness®

Access Consciousness is a set of tools, techniques, systems and philosophy that will change any part of your life that isn't working the way you'd like it to. Access is designed to empower you to create the life you desire. The aim of Access is to create a world of consciousness and oneness, where everything exists and nothing is judged.

For more information, go here:
www.accessconsciousness.com

Access Bars® Class

The first class in Access is Access Bars®. There are 32 points on your head which, when gently touched, effortlessly and easily release anything that doesn't allow you to receive. It's like hitting the delete button on your computer.

For more information, go here:
accessconsciousness.com/accessbars

Talk To The Entities® (TTTE)

Talk To The Entities is a specialty class of Access Consciousness. Talk To The Entities® is aimed at creating more consciousness and awareness around entities, spirits and ghosts and the way people interact and communicate with them.

What would it be like if there were no more fear and judgment in regards to entities but rather an easy, rewarding reality where people and entities were in total allowance of one another?

Shannon O' Hara- Founder, Talk To The Entities: https://www.talktotheentities.com/about-talk-to-the-entities/

InnerDance

InnerDance is not a physical dance as such. The dance happens inside of us. It's an immersive, energetic sound journey that weaves frequencies, energies, rhythms & sounds together. It's a Sound & Sensory Healing Journey. The Inner Dance process helps us peel away the layers of our conditioned mental limitations. It can slowly reveal our deeper core principles and our primary reason for existing on the planet.

Find more about InnerDance with Amy here: www.amyshine.net/innerdance

Ecstatic Chakra Dance

Ecstatic Chakra Dance: is a powerful way to bypass the thinking mind and tap straight into the wisdom of the body. The dance is based on Somatic Embodiment practices that bring our conscious awareness from the mind down into the body so we can move from a place of sensation and feeling instead of thinking. Our dance doesn't have choreography or steps to learn so there's no way to do it wrong. Ecstatic Dance is a free form movement practice that is done with intention. The dance will begin slow, and build up to peak intensity and then come back down into stillness. We use sound, breath, and embodiment movement practices to move you through the chakras.

For more information, go here: www.amyshine.net/movement

www.ingramcontent.com/pod-product-compliance
Lightning Source LLC
Chambersburg PA
CBHW032035090426
42741CB00006B/825